BULLS EYE

THE STEP-BY-STEP PROCESS OF THE MOST POWERFUL
GOAL-SETTING PROCESS
TO ACHIEVING ANY GOAL

By
ERIC LOFHOLM
AUTHOR OF *THE SYSTEM*

DEDICATION:
Bulls Eye is dedicated to my parents.
Because my parents remarried, I have four parents. My father Paul Lofholm, my stepmother Rebecca Lofholm, my mother Diana Jordan and my stepfather Steve Jordan all have been incredible role models in my life. I have been blessed and continue to be blessed with strong family support.

Copyright ©2007-2015 Eric Lofholm International, LLC
All rights reserved. Written permission must be secured from the publisher to use or reproduce any part of this book, except for brief quotations in critical reviews or articles.

This publication is designed to provide accurate and authoritative information in regard to the subject matter covered. It is sold with the understanding that the publisher is not engaged in rendering legal, accounting, or other professional service. If legal advice or other expert assistance is required, the services of a professional should be sought.

Lofholm, Eric
Bulls Eye: The Step-by-Step Process of the Most Powerful Goal-Setting Process to Achieving Any Goal
ISBN-13: 978-1508528944
ISBN-10: 1508528942
Goal Setting
Eric Lofholm International, Inc.
Rocklin, California
916.626.6820
www.ericlofholm.com

ACKNOWLEDGMENTS

I wish to thank many people who have made this book possible. First, my wife, Jarris, who took my ideas and brought them to life in this book. She has played a huge role in my life in helping me bring my ideas to written form.

I wish to thank Andrew Duggan and Ken McGee. They have been instrumental in my development of the goal-setting process revealed in this book. Over one year before the publication of this book, Andrew and I talked about creating a computer program on goal setting. With the help of the principles in this book, we turned that idea into reality. And that is what this book is about – to give you the tools to turn your dreams into reality.

In appreciation,
Eric Lofholm

BULLS EYE

INTRODUCTION

This book is probably the smallest book ever written exclusively on the subject of goals, but don't let the size fool you. This book is very likely the most powerful book ever written on the subject of goals. Goal setting is perhaps the most widely endorsed personal development idea in the world. Consider the following people who endorse goal setting: Oprah Winfrey, Michael Jordan, Pat Summit, Mark McGwire, Zig Ziglar, Napoleon Hill and Jim Carrey.

Goal setting is also one of the most misunderstood personal development ideas. I attended a personal development seminar recently. There were over 1000 people in attendance. The speaker shared his insight into goal setting. What he shared and what I learned I found fascinating; I think you will find it fascinating as well. The speaker asked the group, "How many of you consider yourselves goal setters?" 99% of the people in the audience raised their hands. He then said, "Let's find out. Take out a clean sheet of paper. Write down 10 goals. You have 3 minutes. GO." I began to write. At the end of the 3 minutes I only had 7 goals. I was surprised I was not able to come up with 10. The speaker then asked the group, "How many of you were able to come up with 10 goals?" About 50 hands went up. Remember, there were over 1000 people in the room. Only 5% were able to complete this simple exercise. He then went on to say that the reason most of us were unable to complete the exercise was because we are not goal setters. He continued, "For a goal to be a goal, it must be written down. Most people think that goal setting is merely deciding what you want. That is only the first step. Goal setting is a process.

If you are not following the process, then what you are doing is not goal setting." He went on to teach us his process. I was fascinated because all along I thought I was goal setting, and I realized in that moment that I wasn't. Since that day, I have been working on creating my own goal-setting process. I quickly looked for all for the goal setting information I could find in books, on audio tapes and on videos. From this study I created my own goal-setting process. I created what I believe is the most powerful goal-setting process in the world. This book is designed to influence you to write down your goals and follow the 10-step process that will help you create the life of your dreams.

I designed this book so that you can quickly and easily learn the most successful goal-setting principles in the world.

I will begin by sharing with you why you should set goals and why you should write them down. I will then explain why people don't set goals. I will then teach you my 10-step goal-setting process.

Successfully yours,
Eric

CONTENTS

9 Reasons You Should Set Goals and Write Them Down.. 9
9 Reasons People Don't Set Goals.....................................19
The 10-Step Goal-Setting Process.................................. 29
The Author's Challenge To You....................................41
Appendices.. 43

BULLS EYE

WHY SHOULD I SET GOALS AND WRITE THEM DOWN?

Many people believe they are goal setters, yet they fail to write down their goals. Goal setting is not goal setting unless the goal is written down. Here are 9 reasons you should write down your goals.

9 Reasons You Should Set Goals and Write Them Down.

1. Written goals help you reduce stress by creating a compelling future for you.
2. Written goals point you in the direction you want to take.
3. Written goals activate your subconscious mind.
4. Written goals help you clearly communicate your life plans to others.
5. Written goals increase the likelihood that you will accomplish your goals by 1000%.
6. Written goals improve your time management skills.
7. Written goals motivate you.
8. Written goals help you manage the coincidences in your life.
9. Written goals help you create the life of your dreams.

1. Written goals help you reduce stress by creating a compelling future for you.

What causes stress? I have often thought about that question. My answer is that stress is caused by fear of the future. What if you had no fear of the future, would you have stress? My answer is no.

Written goals will help you reduce stress by creating a compelling future for you. Have you ever met a negative person? I know I have. For many years I wondered what the difference is between a positive and negative person. My answer is what they believe about their futures. Negative people tend to predict negative futures. Positive people tend to predict positive futures. The future is imaginary. It exists only in our imagination. Because the future is imaginary, then why not imagine a bright, compelling future. If you have filled your future with all kinds of compelling goals, will you have a bright or dim outlook on the future? Of course, you will have a bright outlook. If you are excited about the future and what it holds for you, will that reduce any fears that you might have about the future?

The answer, of course, is yes. In contrast, if you approach the future with fear and worry, will you probably feel stress about the future? Of course, you will. By having written goals you help reduce stress by creating a compelling future for you.

2. Written goals point you in the direction you want to take.

What would happen if you got in a boat in San Francisco and you had no idea where the boat was going? Where would you end up? The right answer is wherever the boat was going.

Now what if you got to the pier in San Francisco and 3 boats were there? One was a luxury liner headed for Alaska. One was a fishing boat headed for Japan. The last one was a private yacht headed for Los Angeles. You can board any of the 3 boats. Your goal is to get to Japan. Which boat would you board? Of course, the answer is number 2, the fishing boat headed to Japan. Now consider this: The fishing boat is the least luxurious of the 3, and it is the longest ride of the 3. In spite of that, you would take the fishing boat because it would help you reach your destination.

In 5 years you are going to arrive. The question is, "Where?" Written goals point you in the direction you want to take.

3. Written goals activate your subconscious mind.

Have you ever gone to bed, and right before you fell asleep, you were thinking about a problem in your life, and then in the middle of the night, you awoke with the answer?

That is your subconscious mind working for you. Another example is when the server asks you for your drink order at a restaurant. Do you find yourself telling the server what you want to drink without thinking about it? When you eat you might always drink Coke, coffee, water or iced tea, so you order that drink without thinking about it. This is an example of your subconscious mind working.

An iceberg is a great metaphor for the power of your subconscious mind. When you are on the surface of the water, you can see the tip of the iceberg – your conscious mind. If you go under the water, though, you will see a much larger mass of ice – your subconscious mind. Your subconscious mind has a tremendous influence on your behavior.

Another example of how your subconscious mind works is smoking. Many people smoke unconsciously. Obviously smoking is not a good habit to have, but let's look at the concept of habits. What if you could program good habits into your subconscious mind and use them without thinking about it, as the smoker does with cigarettes? One way to enter thought into your subconscious mind is by following my 10-step goal-setting process. I don't really understand how it works. I just know from my own experience and from the experience of others that it does work. I will say it again.
I don't really understand how it works. I just know that it does work. Written goals activate your subconscious mind.

4. Written goals help you clearly communicate your life plans to others.

Many of the goals you have will require the assistance and cooperation of others. One skill you will need to develop is the ability to clearly communicate your goals to others. When you go through the process of writing down your goals, you are improving your ability to communicate your goals to yourself. Once you have clearly communicated your goals to yourself, you will automatically improve your ability to communicate your goals to others.

5. Written goals increase the likelihood that you will accomplish your goals by 1000%.

A great example to which many people can relate is a wedding. When you planned your wedding, did you write down your goals?
Chances are you did. And do you believe that effort increased the probability that your wedding plans would be realized? Without the written goals, the overall plan for the wedding would have been lost.

6. Written goals improve your time management skills.

Goals give your life direction. When you have direction, you know where to focus your time and energy. If your goal is to become the top real estate agent in your area, are you likely to have a job as a receptionist? No, of course not; you would have a job as a real estate agent. My point is many people have jobs that are not helping them achieve their dreams because they have never taken the time to think about what they want and write it down. Written goals give a clear idea of the best ways you can invest your time.

7. Written goals motivate you.

I am a sales coach. I have met thousands of salespeople who hate to make cold calls. On a scale of 1 to 10, their motivation to make sales calls is 1. I have also met many salespeople who are extremely motivated to make cold calls.

What is the difference between the two? I have found that the motivated salespeople focus on the benefit they are receiving by making the cold calls. In other words, they have invested time to clearly communicate to themselves the specific benefits they are receiving by making the calls. When you have written goals, you have a plan in writing that communicates to you the benefits you are going to receive once you take action. Written goals motivate you.

8. Written goals help you manage the coincidences in your life.

Have you ever had a goal and the goal manifested itself by coincidence? Here is an example that happened to my wife and me recently. When we moved into our house, we wanted to get a new kitchen table. Within 30 days of writing down that goal, our friend, Mark, offered us a brand new kitchen table with 4 matching chairs for **free.** The table, had we bought it new, would have cost over $1,000. Events like this happen every day. When I am very clear on what I want and follow the 10-step goal-setting process, I find it to be true that coincidences like that happen all the time. I feel it is a way to influence luck. Test it out. Become clear on what you want, follow the 10-step goal-setting process and see what happens. Now I am not suggesting that you don't take consistent action. I am saying that sometimes results come without effort, as in my example above. Written goals help you manage the coincidences in your life.

9. Written goals help you create the life of your dreams.

Why did you purchase this book? Why are you investing the time to learn these proven principles? For most people the answer is to help you create the life of your dreams.

Show me a successful person, and I will show you how she is applying these proven principles in her life. Goal setting is quite possibly the most endorsed personal development strategy in the world. Consider the following list of people who endorse goal setting: Oprah Winfrey, Michael Jordan, Pat Summitt, Rick Pitino, Mark Victor Hansen, Napoleon Hill, Zig Ziglar, Andrew Carnegie, Thomas Edison, Tom Hopkins, Jim Carrey, Arnold Schwarzenegger, Tiger Woods, Rickey Henderson. All of these people believe in goal-setting principles. Show me a successful person, and I will show you a goal setter. The results speak for themselves.

These principles are like gravity. If you are holding a cup of coffee and you drop the cup, what happens? Right, the cup breaks and coffee goes everywhere. If you drop the cup, will the cup always fall? The answer is yes. 100% of the time the cup will fall. That is because of the law of gravity. The goal setting principles I have in this program are proven – like gravity. If you apply the 10-step goal-setting process, it will help you achieve your goals. If you want to create the life of your dreams, then you must first clearly define *then life of your dreams.* Then you must write it down. Then you must create a plan of action. Then you must take action. Written goals help you create the life of your dreams.

WHY DON'T PEOPLE SET GOALS?

By now you clearly see the benefits of goal setting. You realize that this is the one strategy consistently used by the most successful people in the world. You might be asking yourself, "So why doesn't everyone use goal setting as a strategy to realize their dreams?" Here are the 9 reasons people don't set goals.

9 Reasons People Don't Set Goals

1. They don't know the importance of goal setting.
2. They don't know how.
3. They think they are already doing it.
4. They don't have any goals.
5. They are afraid of failure. By not setting a goal, there is no way to fail.
6. They don't believe in themselves. Achieving a goal is not a possibility in their minds.
7. They suffer from the curse of early success.
8. They are in a comfort zone.
9. They are afraid of success.

1. They don't know the importance of goal setting.

Is it possible to become a millionaire without setting a goal of being a millionaire? The answer, of course, is yes. One example of how you could accomplish that is to inherit a million dollars. Another example is for you to win the lottery. What are the chances that you will inherit one million dollars or win the lottery? Not very high. The chances of your becoming a millionaire without making it a goal are very slim.

Goal setting is important because by setting goals you dramatically increase the chances of your getting out of life everything that you want. The main benefit of goal setting is that it will help you get anything you want in life faster and easier than without goals. Once people realize how important goal setting is, they immediately become goal setters.

2. They don't know how.

Where did you learn how to set goals? How effective was the teacher, the book or the tape at teaching you the fundamental principles of goal setting? Most people have never been taught proper goal-setting techniques. A simple analogy to illustrate this point is a person who doesn't ski.

The number one reason people don't ski is that they don't know how. Many people don't set goals because they don't know how.

3. They think they are already doing it.

Many people think they are already setting goals. In fact you may be one of those people. You might have gone through your life until now believing that you were already using proper goal-setting techniques. Consider the following example: a high school student might set the goal to have a GPA of 3.5. This is a fairly gifted student who, if he truly applied himself, could have a 4.0 GPA. At the beginning of the semester, his parents asked him what his GPA goal was for the semester. He responded with "3.5." His parents were satisfied with the answer and moved on to the next topic.

The problem is that is not goal setting. The end of the story is that he finished the semester with a 3.0 GPA. There is nothing wrong with a B average. The problem is he wanted a 3.5. That was his goal, and his academic ability was a 4.0.

If he had followed proper goal-setting techniques, he probably would have exceeded his goal. He goes through life thinking goal setting is merely deciding what he wants.

Deciding what you want is just one of many steps. There are 9 other specific steps that must be taken to provide the best opportunity for success. Think about it; how many times have you known what you wanted and come up short? How much more successful would you be right now if you had been taught proper goal-setting techniques in junior high school and high school?

4. They don't have any goals.

Over the last 10 years I have met several people who tell me they don't have any goals. If you ask these people what their goals are, they respond by saying they don't have any.

This is not really true, though. They do have goals; they just have never taken the time to think about what they really want in life. Whenever I ask people who say they don't have any goals, "Would you like to retire financially independent?"

What do you think they say? Of course, they say yes. Or I will ask them, "Would you like to have more energy? Would you like to make more money? Would you like to get a promotion at your job?"

They always respond by saying yes. Everyone has goals. Yet not everyone has taken the time to really think about what they want most in life, then write it down, then create a plan for achievement and then take action.

5. They are afraid of failure.

Have you ever met someone who enjoys the experience of failure? I surely haven't. We all want to succeed in life. Many people are so afraid of failing that they are afraid of trying. They have the goal, the vision and the dream in their minds, but they never take action because the thought of failure dominates their minds. If you fall into this category, my suggestion to you is to set small goals using proper goal-setting techniques. Once your confidence is up and you see how easy it is, you can move on to bigger goals.

Also keep in mind, there is risk in everything. There is risk in going after your goals. (What if I fail?) There is also risk in not going after your goals. (What if I get through my life without going after what was most important to me?) For me,

I would rather pursue my dream and fail than go through life asking, "What if?"

6. They don't believe in themselves.

If you believe that you don't have the talent to write a book, would you ever set a goal to write a book? Probably not. Our beliefs shape our behavior. In most cases we will only attempt what we believe we can achieve. For some people this fact limits their experience. Every time they think of a compelling goal that excites them, they tell themselves, "I could never do that." Yes, you can do that and much more. Goal setting is not a belief exercise. I will say it again.

Goal setting is not a belief exercise. Goal setting is an exercise in clearly defining what you want, writing it down, creating a plan for achievement and taking action. The process of goal setting is not a belief exercise. For some people, once they grasp that, the light bulb goes on. They think, "I thought I had to believe I could achieve the goal before I set it. Now that I know the process does not have belief as a prerequisite, I can do it."

7. They suffer from the curse of early success.

Some people achieve success at an early age. They leave high school or college, and no one has told them yet that they can't achieve great things in their lives. They try different things and success comes easily to them. And then life deals them a blow, as life does.

All of a sudden success doesn't come so easily. In fact, they lose the success they had. They lose their companies. They go bankrupt. They get divorced.

They lose that unstoppable confidence they had, and they stop setting goals. What goals have you given up? When do you tell yourself you are too old, not smart enough, not talented enough, without enough time, without enough money? Whatever reason you have for not succeeding, I can show you someone who has faced greater adversity and succeeded.

8. They are in a comfort zone.

Many people are comfortable where they are in their lives. They have no desire to strive for more out of life. I accept that answer. There is nothing that says we need to constantly be striving for more. However, I have one question for a person who is in the *comfort zone*. Do you truly have what you want out of life, or are you settling for less?

9. They are afraid of success.

What if you had a big goal such as becoming CEO of a Fortune 500 company? This goal is appealing to you because you would be the boss. You would make an extraordinary income. Then you start thinking, "Yeah, what if I became a CEO? What about all of that responsibility? What about all that stress?" All of a sudden you become fearful of the consequences of success. Here is the question: If a person fears what will happen if he succeeds, how likely will he be to get started? Do you have goals that you are not pursuing because you fear the consequences if you succeed?

INTRODUCTION TO SETTING GOALS

I believe the 10-step goal-setting process I am going to share with you is the most effective goal-setting process in the world. When I designed this process, I wanted to combine the most effective goal-setting strategies with the easiest application. While I was creating this system, many of the processes I looked at were either too complicated or didn't give you enough information to be effective. The following system is designed with you in mind. Follow the 10 simple steps in order, and turn your dreams into reality.

The 10-Step Goal-Setting Process

1. Think about what you want, and write it down.
2. Decide **exactly** what you want, and write it down.
3. Make sure your goal is measurable.
4. Identify the specific reasons you want this goal, and write them down.
5. Establish a definite date for accomplishment of your goal, and write it down.
6. List the action steps you need to take to accomplish your goal, and write them down.
7. Create an action plan from your list of action steps, and write it down.
8. Take action.
9. Do something every day.
10. View your goals as often as possible.

1. Think about what you want, and write it down.

What is your dream? Where do you want to travel in your lifetime? How much money do you want to have when you retire? What would be the ideal job? The goal-setting process starts with thinking about what you want and how you want your life to be. One simple way to think is to ask questions. I have learned that your mind works like a search engine on the Internet. When you are on the Internet, you might go to a search engine such as Yahoo. On Yahoo you can search for websites just like you can search for companies in a phone book. When you make a search on Yahoo, you type in the word and Yahoo will search for matching websites. Your brain is a search engine. When you ask it a question such as,
"What would be the ideal job?" your brain will search through its files and produce an answer. One way to effectively think about what you want is to ask yourself questions about what you want. When you get the answers, write them down. There is no right way to think about what you want. The ideas will become a menu of choices from which you can create your goals. We call this menu the thought menu. You want as many choices as possible.

While I teach you the 10-step goal-setting process, I want to show you an example of what I mean. The example will be a health goal. Assume I am a person who wants to lose weight. I have low energy. I currently weigh 238. I have poor eating habits. During this brainstorming session I will ask myself several health-related questions to create my thought menu. Here are 4 examples of questions I will ask: How do I want to feel when I wake up in the morning? What would my ideal weight be? What type of food do I want to put into my body? What foods should I be avoiding? My answers are as follows: I want to feel energized when I wake up in the morning. My ideal body weight is 185 pounds. I want to eat more fruits and vegetables. I should avoid fast food, ice cream and soda. These answers become my thought menu.

2. Decide exactly what you want and write it down.

Look at your thought menu. From this menu of ideas, take each idea to its completion. The second step in goal setting is to decide exactly what you want. Be as specific as you can. For example, "I want to earn $100,000 over the next 12 months." Notice, my goal was not, "I want to make more money next year." That would not be specific enough. From our example I look at my thought menu.

- I want to feel energized when I wake up in the morning.
- My ideal body weight is 185 pounds.
- I want to eat more fruits and vegetables.
- I will avoid fast food, ice cream and soda.

From the thought menu I want to take the idea to its completion. I decide the specific goal I want is to weigh 185 pounds. I now weigh 238. My goal is to lose 53 pounds.

3. Make sure your goal is measurable.

For a goal to be a goal, it must be written down. Once you have written it down, look at your goal to see if it is measurable. What I mean by measurable is that you will know when you have accomplished your goal. In our example my goal is to weigh 185 pounds or to lose 53 pounds. It is measurable, so it passes the test. If my goal were not measurable, then I would go back to Step 2 and rewrite the goal, making sure that it is measurable.

4. Identify the specific reasons you want this goal, and write them down.

The reason most people fail to achieve their goals is that they don't have a compelling enough reason to achieve them.

Once you have begun the 10-step goal-setting process, you are ready to take action. Along the path toward achieving your goals, you are going to run into some obstacles. That is where your **why** comes in. If your reason for achieving the goal is greater than the obstacles you face, then you will be much more likely to achieve the goal. Here is an example:

You have been smoking a pack of cigarettes per day for 18 years. You have had a goal to quit smoking for the last 6 years because you know smoking isn't good for you. You followed proper goal-setting techniques. You tried hypnosis, gum and quit-smoking seminars. Nothing seems to work. You go to the doctor. The doctor says you have lung cancer. If you quit smoking now you will have 10 years to live. If you keep smoking you will die in 1 year.

Would you be able to quit smoking? I think most people would. Even though it was a goal of yours for the last 6 years, and you were unable to succeed, I believe most people would be able to quit.

They have a strong enough reason to accomplish the goal. When you set a goal, look at **why** you want to achieve the goal. Is your **why** a big enough reason for you to overcome the obstacles to achieving your goal? If you don't have a strong enough reason, then imagine one. Spend some time really thinking about what it would mean to you to accomplish the goal. Also think about what the consequences will be if you don't accomplish the goal.

Write a paragraph about **why** you will succeed in achieving your goal. Once you have completed the paragraph, read it over. After reading the paragraph, ask yourself the question, "Do I have a big enough **why** to overcome the obstacles I am going to encounter?"

Back to my weight-loss example. Here is my **why**: I must lose 53 pounds because this is not the person I really am. I am sick and tired of people thinking of me as fat. I want to run a marathon before I die, and I will never be able to do it at this weight.

I then look at my **why** paragraph. I believe I have a strong enough **why** to overcome the obstacles I am going to face, so I continue with the process. If my **why** is not compelling enough, I must go back and rewrite it.

5. Establish a definite date for accomplishment of your goal, and write it down.

It is very important to decide when you want to accomplish your goal. Your mind has an unconscious time line in it. For example, if your goal is to graduate from college by the end of 2018, your mind needs to start working on plans for how you will graduate in 2018. Knowing when you want to accomplish your goal will also have an effect on how you plan to achieve your goal. For example, if your goal is to earn $100,000 in the next 12 months, that is very different from having a goal of earning $100,000 any time in the future.

Once you write down a date for your goal, your mind will start working toward achieving your goal. The only way to take advantage of your mind is to set a date and enter it into your subconscious by writing it down. In our weight-loss example, my goal was to lose 53 pounds by March 25, 2016.

6. List the action steps you need to take to accomplish your goal, and write them down.

Ask yourself "What are all of the steps I need to take to accomplish my goal?" This is a brainstorming exercise.

Here we are looking to capture as many ideas as possible. We call this the action steps menu. Once again, we want as many choices as possible to create our plan. We are not looking for the steps to be in order at this point. Take out a clean sheet of paper and write anything and everything that comes to mind – things you will need to do in order to achieve your goal. Here is my action steps menu for our weight loss example:

- Go to the health food store to get good food.
- Exercise 3 times per week.
- Take a multi-vitamin every day.
- Meet with a nutrition expert to establish a diet.
- Meet with an exercise specialist to create a workout program.
- Create a tracking system to track my results.
- Buy an exercise book.
- Talk to my friend Bob (Bob lost 30 pounds last year) to find out how he lost weight.

Notice that the list is not in any particular order. This is a brainstorming session. I am looking to capture as many ideas as I can on paper. Once I have listed as many ideas as I can think of, I will then go to the next step.

7. Create an action plan from your list of action steps, and write it down.

Step 7 is where your thoughts mesh into a plan. Look at your action steps from **Step 6.** Put those ideas in sequential order. First do this. Then do that. All we are doing to create our plan is to prioritize the action steps in **Step 6.** Do not let the word plan scare you. This is a simple exercise.

1. Talk to my friend Bob (Bob lost 30 pounds last year) and find out how he lost weight.
2. Buy an exercise book.
3. Make an appointment to meet with a nutrition expert to establish a diet.
4. Make an appointment to meet with an exercise specialist to create a workout plan.
5. Meet with the nutrition expert.
6. Go to the health food store to get good food.
7. Take a multi-vitamin every day.
8. Meet with the exercise specialist.
9. Create a tracking system to track my results.
10. Exercise 3 times per week.

When many people think about creating an action plan, they think of a lengthy process. The word *plan* scares them.

As you can see from the above example, the plan took only a few minutes of thought. When you create a plan to achieve a goal, you need to ask yourself, "If I follow the plan, will

I achieve the goal?" So in our example, if we execute the plan, would we lose 53 pounds in 2 years? The answer is yes.

8. Take action.

Every step in the 10-step goal-setting process is important. Each step depends upon the others. This step, however, could be the most important. I can't tell you how many educated derelicts I have met over the years – you know, the person who knows everything about everything, yet can't seem to get himself to take action on his own life.

Goals and plans are great, but they don't produce results.
The only thing that produces results is action. How many times have you planned to do something, yet when it came to the action phase, you didn't act? You must get yourself to take consistent action on a daily basis – even if they are baby steps. Remember:

Inch by inch, it's a cinch. When you take action on a consistent basis, even if it is a small step, you take advantage of the law of momentum. The law of momentum states that a body in motion, once in motion, tends to stay in motion.

In our weight-loss example, one action I might take today is to go to the health food store and pick out some food.

That is a positive step toward the achievement of my goal.
It is a small step. This step will help me create momentum.

Another step I might take is to jog for 2 minutes today. That might not seem like a lot, but it really is. Most people never achieve their goals because they never take the first step.

They never benefit from the law of momentum. Remember, the journey of a thousand miles begins with just one step.
Inch by inch, it's a cinch.

9. Do something every day.

Work toward the achievement of your goals every day – even if it is a small step. Rome wasn't built in a day, and your major life goals aren't going to happen overnight in most cases. Practice patience.

In our weight-loss example, "Today I will make an appointment with Bob to find out how he was able to lose the weight." This action is a small step toward the achievement of my goal. This step will activate the law of momentum. By taking this small step today, I have put the law of momentum in my favor.

10. View your goals as often as possible.

Out of site, out of mind – human beings don't have the best memories. You have invested time to complete **Steps 1 through 9.** Now that your goals are written down with a plan, you can quickly review 5 to 10 goals in a matter of minutes. The more frequently you view your goals, the more you will burn them into your subconscious mind. Something magical happens when you do that. After some time of frequently reviewing your goals with their plans of action, your subconscious mind will start to believe you are going to achieve the goal. Once you have accomplished that, you can take advantage of the most powerful personal development idea ever discovered. **We become what we think about.**

Notice, with the exception of **Step 8** *(take action),* every step requires that you think about what you want. Remember: **We become what we think about.** This is one of the secrets of this 10-step process. The process requires that you invest time thinking about what you want most in your life. Many people who do not achieve their goals invest their time thinking of all the reasons they can never succeed in their lives, or they invest their time thinking of ways to solve other peoples' problems, or they invest their thinking time in the fact that they have no money. Note there is nothing wrong with thinking about these things. However, if you choose to invest your time thinking in that way, just realize the consequences. Remember: **We become what we think about.**

THE AUTHOR'S CHALLENGE TO YOU

You have just learned the most powerful goal-setting process in the world. I challenge you to take action – to implement these proven principles and create the life of your dreams.

BULLS EYE

APPENDIX A

9 Reasons You Should Set Goals and Write Them Down

1. Written goals help you reduce stress by creating a compelling future for you.
2. Written goals point you in the direction you want to take.
3. Written goals activate your subconscious mind.
4. Written goals help you clearly communicate your life plans to others.
5. Written goals increase the likelihood that you will accomplish your goals by 1000%.
6. Written goals improve your time management skills.
7. Written goals motivate you.
8. Written goals help you manage the coincidences in your life.
9. Written goals help you create the life of your dreams.

Appendix B

9 Reasons People Don't Set Goals

1. They don't know the importance of goal setting.
2. They don't know how.
3. They think they are already doing it.
4. They don't have any goals.
5. They are afraid of failure. By not setting a goal, there is no way to fail.
6. They don't believe in themselves. Achieving a goal is not a possibility in their minds.
7. They suffer from the curse of early success.
8. They are in a comfort zone.
9. They are afraid of success.

Appendix C

The 10-Step Goal-Setting Process

1. Think about what you want, and write it down.
2. Decide **exactly** what you want, and write it down.
3. Make sure your goal is measurable.
4. Identify the specific reasons you want this goal, and write them down.
5. Establish a definite date for accomplishment of your goal, and write it down.
6. List the action steps you need to take to accomplish your goal, and write them down.
7. Create an action plan from your list of action steps, and write it down.
8. Take action.
9. Do something every day.
10. View your goals as often as possible.

BULLS EYE

About the Author:

Eric Lofholm is a master sales trainer who has helped over 10,000 students make more sales. Trained by best-selling sales expert Dr. Donald Moine, Eric has helped generate nearly $500 million in revenue in the last two decades. Eric hones his skills as a sales trainer for Tony Robbins from 1997 to 1999 before founding his own company, Eric Lofholm International. He offers expert training for both corporate sales departments and for individuals who want to improve their sales skills.

He is the author of the #1 best-selling book *The System*. You can get your copy at: http://www.amazon.com/System-Proven-3-Step-Formula-Appointments/dp/0989894207/ref=sr_1_1?ie=UTF8&qid=1421081452&sr=8-1&keywords=Eric+Lofholm+The+System
Eric is also the publisher of the I Love Selling Magazine and the I Love Selling Podcast. He is the father of two children.

Visit Eric's web site at www.SalesChampion.com

CPSIA information can be obtained at www.ICGtesting.com
Printed in the USA
LVOW04s1334190315

431235LV00017B/302/P